KT-495-451

The Publishers gratefully acknowledge assistance provided by Sir Penius Wroughshod, F.B.S.H., Executive Secretary of the British Society of Husbands, in compiling this book.

Publishers: Ladybird Books Ltd, Loughborough

Printed in England. If wet, Italy.

'How it works'

THE
HUSBAND

by J. A. HAZELEY, N.S.F.W.
and J. P. MORRIS, O.M.G.

(Authors of 'Eat Yourself Fat')

A LADYBIRD BOOK FOR GROWN-UPS

This is a husband.

He may look complicated, but he is in fact very simple.

He runs on sausages and beer.

The husband knows many things.

For example, he knows how many stairs there are, in case he arrives home unable to see them properly.

The husband likes to do simple repairs, like changing the washer on a tap.

Afterwards he likes to talk at great length about what a struggle it was, and will want to be treated as if he has invented a machine that turns farts into gold.

The husband has a very big memory. He can remember football scores, all his old car number plates, and most of the film *Withnail & I*.

But he cannot remember what his wife asked him to bring back from the shops. This is because his brain is full up, not because he was not listening.

On special occasions, the husband and wife dress up to go out together.

Emma has lots of outfits. Graham has one suit. It is called His Suit, and he has had it for a long time.

Graham likes His Suit, even though it has not fitted in years, has a four-inch gusset rip and makes him look like a burglar in court.

The husband finds some things very difficult. Being wrong is one of these things.

When he is wrong, the husband will refer to the times he was right, even if they date back many years.

It is important for the husband to pretend that he had no life before he was married, especially if he was married before he was married.

Jimbo works hard all week and only has a few hours at the weekend to spend with his family.

He spends these hours watching sport.

The wife likes to read romantic fiction. The books are a fantasy and an escape for her.

The husband does not waste his time on silly stories. He likes to read books about things that really happened and tales of real men.

Reading these will be invaluable if he ever has to land on the moon or be in the S.A.S. or help manage the England football team.

This is what the inside of Tim's head looks like.

It also contains pictures of some ladies before they have put their clothes on.

None of the ladies is Tim's wife.

The husband always has the right tool for the job.

A screwdriver in the kitchen for opening pickled onions.

A shoe on the sideboard for putting up pictures.

And a bread knife in the lavatory for dispatching monsters.

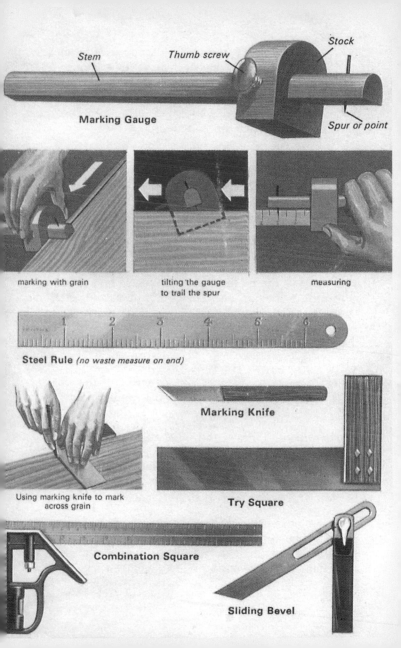

Marking Gauge

Stem *Thumb screw* *Stock* *Spur or point*

marking with grain

tilting the gauge to trail the spur

measuring

Steel Rule *(no waste measure on end)*

1   2   3   4   5   6

Using marking knife to mark across grain

Marking Knife

Try Square

Combination Square

Sliding Bevel

The husband finds it difficult to express his feelings, so at this men's talking therapy group, husbands are encouraged to open up.

Three of these husbands are playing poker and one of them is reading a book about ghosts.

They are not talking.

In Japan, you can buy a robot husband.

This is M1, a fully motorised electronic husband. He can move furniture, barbecue, clear gutters, carve roast dinners, install TVs, kick and catch balls, and is even programmed to apologise.

Sadly, scientists cannot work out how to stop him burping.

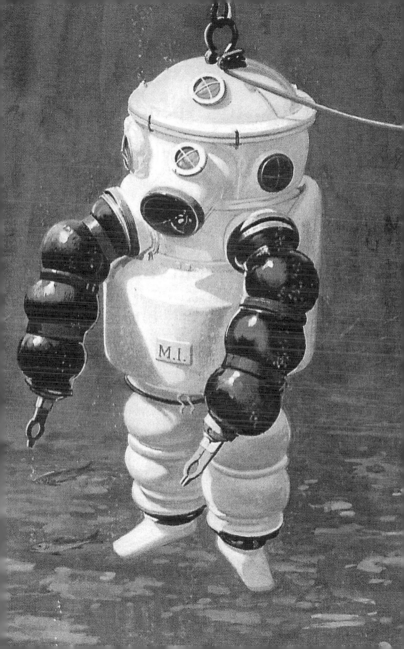

Glyn explains himself very badly.

This is so he can say he is misunderstood.

Husbands like to meet with friends for a chat.

This husband has been talking to his friends for five and a half hours about which Doctor Who would win in a game of hide-and-seek.

He has forgotten to ask whether his friends' wives and children are still living with them, or even alive.

As the husband grows older, he starts to make lots of funny little noises.

He sighs as he gets out of a chair, and talks like Inspector Clouseau when he feels conversation has dried up.

He also pom-pom-poms as he goes from room to room.

This is to remind himself that he's still here.

Nerys and Ross are now the parents of a baby boy. Ross was there for the birth. Nerys would have preferred him to be here, but he was there.

Nerys is delighted to be a mum, and cannot stop looking at her newborn.

Ross is looking at the nurses.

Husbands like nurses.

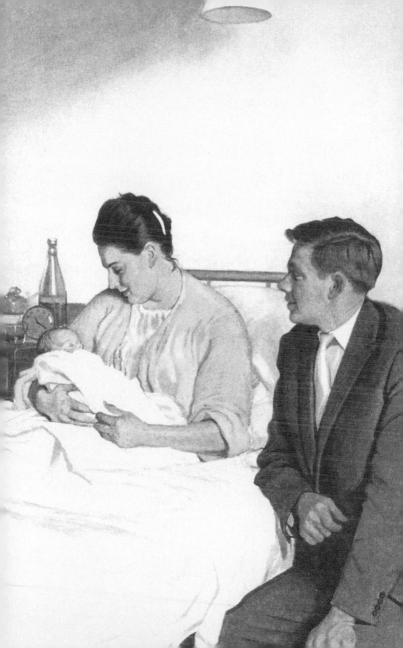

Helen complains that Stuart spends too much time on his computer and telephone.

"Let's have a family Sunday without them," says Helen. "Just you, me and Sally."

Stuart has bought a newspaper that weighs more than Sally.

"Shh," says Stuart.

Nigel is out for a picnic with his wife and children. The au pair has also come along.

Nigel has to sit with one leg up to disguise the unfortunate way that the au pair brings out the beast in him.

Hugh moved to the country to give his family a better life.

His journey to work in the city now takes three hours each way.

He is only at home when his wife and children are asleep, which has given them all a better life.

Jim has just found all the clutch bags he has bought his wife as Christmas and birthday presents. She said she lost them, but she has hidden them in the loft.

Jim and Rebecca have been husband and wife for thirty-one years and he still does not know what she likes.

This Christmas, he will probably get her another bag just the same.

Husbands like do-it-yourself.

Today, Richard has hung a door so it gets stuck on the hall carpet and built a flat-pack chest of drawers with three mysterious metal shapes left over – and he did it all by himself.

Now he is repeatedly driving up and down the same half-mile stretch of road and not asking directions himself.

PRIVATE

The husband hears as much as 30% of what is said to him.

Many husbands are traditional and do not believe in listening before marriage.

VIBRATING
HAMMER, ANVIL
AND
STIRRUP

SENSE OF
BALANCE
CANALS

MEMBRANE

AUDITORY
CANAL

EAR DRUM

MIDDLE EAR

BLUE AREA INDICATES
FLUID FILLED INNER
EAR

The husband likes things to be in order. At home, the DVDs, spanners, shirts, golf clubs, wine, spare lightbulbs and the kitchen knives are in an order that the husband understands.

Adrian is putting his family's shoes in alphabetical order. This will make them harder to find, but at least it will be logical.

Adrian's wife sometimes cries herself to sleep.

The authors would like to thank the illustrators whose work they have so mercilessly
ribbed, and whose glorious craftsmanship was the set-dressing of their childhoods.
The inspiration they sparked has never faded.

MICHAEL JOSEPH

UK | USA | Canada | Ireland | Australia
India | New Zealand | South Africa

Michael Joseph is part of the Penguin Random House group of companies
whose addresses can be found at global.penguinrandomhouse.com

Penguin
Random House
UK

First published 2015
009

Copyright © Jason Hazeley and Joel Morris, 2015
All images copyright © Ladybird Books Ltd, 2015

The moral right of the authors has been asserted

Printed in Italy by L.E.G.O. S.p.A

A CIP catalogue record for this book is available from the British Library

ISBN: 978–0–718–18356–1

www.greenpenguin.co.uk